watercress

First published in Great Britain in 2008
by WA Publishing, WAPR, Regal House, Twickenham

ISBN 978-0-9558 126-0-6

Researched and compiled by Wendy Akers
Funded by The Watercress Alliance (Vitacress Salads, Alresford Salads, The Watercress Company)
Historic photographs: Bill Jesty

Food photography: Frank Adam and James Duncan
Farm photography: William Shaw and Ludwig Haskins
Recipes (excluding Antony Worrall Thompson's): Jane Lawrie

Designed and produced by SP Creative Design
Editor: Heather Thomas
Designer: Rolando Ugolini

Printed and bound in Singapore by Star Standard Pte Ltd

Note
Salt which has been added for seasoning purposes has not been included in the salt content in the recipes' nutritional analysis.

contents

a rich culinary history

Watercress is a fantastic salad leaf. Its lush, plump, vibrant leaves not only taste wonderfully peppery, but they are amazingly good for us too, brimming with vitamins and minerals. As a chef, I love the versatility of watercress. The classic watercress dish is soup – velvety, rich and emerald green, it tastes as good as it looks.

For centuries, watercress was a winter crop. As with oysters, you were advised to eat it only if there was an 'r' in the month, as the plant naturally flowers and runs to seed in the summer. However, by cropping plants before they seed, farmers have transformed watercress into a popular summer salad.

The plant has a natural affinity with citrus fruits, especially orange or grapefruit segments. It also complements the oriental flavours of ginger, chilli and soy, which explains why it is a staple part of the Chinese diet. As you will see from the exciting recipes in this book, watercress can be used in a whole range of dishes, from fish sauces and pesto to stir fries and pasta – the possibilities are endless.

Watercress is part of the UK's rich culinary heritage. In Victorian times, it was often eaten in sandwiches at breakfast time, although in poorer homes it was served on its own, which earned it the nickname 'poor man's bread'. People even thought it was a cure for toothache, hiccups and freckles!

Today, all good chefs include watercress on their menus, while health professionals rave about its amazing nutritional properties and every detox diet includes it. Quite simply, we should all be eating a lot more of it. After years of being dismissed as nothing more than a garnish, watercress is at last achieving the recognition it deserves as the king of salad leaves.

Antony Worrall Thompson

Antony Worrall Thompson

Antony celebrating the start of the British watercress season at The Watercress Festival in Alresford, Hampshire, May 2007.

not just a bit on the side

The vital ingredient for growing watercress is, of course, water – pure, mineral-rich spring water – from which this peppery superfood derives its power house of nutrients. Brimming with more than 15 essential vitamins and minerals, its health-giving properties have been known since ancient times.

A London watercress seller, 1799 (Guildhall Library, City of London)

Gram for gram, watercress contains more vitamin C than oranges, more calcium than milk and more iron than spinach. But people love it for its flavour too. The peppery heat comes from the plant's mustard oils, which are released when chewed and act as a stimulant to digestion and the taste buds, while the stalks are succulent and cool (from the water in which it is grown).

Watercress (*Nasturtium officinale* or *Rorripa nasturtium acquaticum*) has long been an integral ingredient in the British diet, probably because it grew wild in rivers and streams where it could be picked for free (though we don't recommend you do so today). It was used as a cure for all manner of complaints. The herbalist John Gerard thought it could help prevent scurvy while Culpepper claimed that 'watercress potage is a good remedy to cleanse the blood in spring and consume the gross humours winter hath left behind'. In the Stone Age, it was used to make nettle pudding, and the Anglo Saxons even thought it could prevent baldness!

Its heyday was during the Victorian period when the development of the railway allowed tons of the plant to be transported up to London's Covent Garden Market where it was packed into wicker 'flats'. Street sellers would buy it and form it into bunches, which were eaten in the hand, like an ice cream cone – the first 'on the go food'. In 1861, Henry Mayhew noted: 'The first coster cry heard of a morning in the London streets is of "Fresh wo-orter-creases". Those that sell them have to be on their rounds in time for the mechanic's breakfast, or the day's gains are lost'.

Richard Rowe, in 1881, reported: 'In fine weather, in spite of the general squalor of the street-retailers, it is rather a pretty sight to see them flocking out of the great watercress market with their verdant basketfuls and armfuls, freshening their purchases under the sun-gilt water of the pump, splitting them up into bunches, and beautifying the same to the best of their ability to tempt purchasers. The fresh green, and even the litter of picked-off wilted leaves, pleasantly remind one of the country, in the midst of our dusty, dingy, drab wilderness of brick and mortar; and there is something bird-like in the cress-sellers' cry as one after another raises it'.

One watercress seller who made good was Eliza James, who later earned the nickname 'The Watercress Queen' due to her near monopoly of the London watercress restaurant and hotel trade. She created vast watercress beds in Surrey and Hampshire, and, despite her wealth, she still turned up every morning to work her stall at Covent Garden Market, arriving every day on a watercress cart. Reporting on her death in 1927, the *Daily Mirror* described her life as 'one of the most wonderful romances of business London has ever known'.

Bunching watercress in the 1950s.

The watercress industry continued to thrive during both World Wars when the country had to rely on home-grown produce, and watercress sandwiches for 'high tea' became almost a national institution. Watercress was a staple ingredient in school dinners; indeed, several experiments conducted by the Ministry of Health in the 1930s concluded that watercress was excellent for promoting children's growth.

However, the lifting of import restrictions and the introduction of more exotic-looking salad leaves, followed by the closure of many branch railways in the 1960s had a severe effect on the watercress industry and sales declined. In the 1940s, more than 1,000 acres of watercress were under cultivation but by the end of the twentieth century that figure had shrunk to 150 acres. Despite its noble history, watercress was thought of as merely a garnish. However, in 2003, British watercress farmers decided to take action and launched a promotional campaign – 'Not Just a Bit on the Side' – and, as a result, the industry is now enjoying a renaissance, with watercress once again being recognised as the original superfood.

grilled chicken on watercress mash

675g/1¹/₂lb potatoes, peeled

2 (85g) bags watercress, roughly chopped

6 tablespoons 0% fat Greek yoghurt or milk

25g/1oz unsalted butter, diced

pinch of grated nutmeg

75g/3oz watercress butter (see below)

4 x 175g/6oz chicken breast fillets

1 tablespoon olive oil

salt and ground black pepper

For the watercress butter:

1 (85g) bag watercress, finely chopped

75g/3oz unsalted butter, softened

1 shallot, very finely chopped

1 teaspoon English mustard

1 Make the watercress butter: mix the watercress, butter, shallot and mustard together. Season well with black pepper. Keep in the fridge.

2 Cut the potatoes into large chunks, place in a large pan and cover with lightly salted cold water. Cover and bring to the boil, then simmer gently for 10–15 minutes, or until tender. Drain, return to the pan, tip in the chopped watercress and re-cover. Leave to stand for 1–2 minutes, or until the watercress has wilted.

3 Mash the potatoes and watercress, then add the yoghurt or milk and butter. Fluff up with a fork, add the nutmeg and season to taste with ground black pepper. Keep warm.

4 Meanwhile, gently push a little of the watercress butter under the skin of the chicken breast fillets. Preheat a non-stick frying pan. When hot, add the oil, then place the chicken breasts, skin-side down, in the pan and cook for 10–15 minutes, turning once, until the chicken is golden brown on both sides and cooked through.

5 Heap the watercress mash in the centre of 4 warmed plates and top with the chicken. Spoon the pan juices around the chicken and serve, garnished with a sprig of watercress and a wedge of lemon.

Cook's tip
You do not need to use all of the watercress butter. You can use it dabbed onto fish or a steak or even baked potatoes. It will keep for several days in the fridge.

Per serving: calories: 517 fat: 22.6g saturated fat: 11.7g
carbohydrate: 30.6g protein: 49.6g fibre: 3g salt: 0.66g

Preparation: 10 minutes Cooking: 30–35 minutes Serves 4

watercress bubble and squeak

50g/2oz unsalted butter
2 onions, chopped
2 (85g) bags watercress
2 tablespoons vegetable oil
350g/12oz cooked mashed potato
pinch of ground nutmeg
dash of vinegar
4 large eggs
salt and ground black pepper

1 Melt the butter in a non-stick frying pan and then cook the onions over a medium heat for about 5 minutes, until softened but not brown. Chop the watercress, add to the pan and stir fry with the onion until just wilted. Remove from the heat.

2 Heat the oil in a separate pan. Fold the cooked watercress and onion into the mashed potato. Season with salt and pepper and nutmeg and combine everything thoroughly. Turn the mixture into the hot pan and press down to make a circular cake. Cook for 10 minutes over a medium heat without disturbing.

3 Turn the cake over, either by tossing or by sliding it onto a plate and then returning it to the pan. Leave to cook for a further 10 minutes.

4 Meanwhile, poach the eggs: heat 5cm/2ins of water in a non-stick frying pan. Add the vinegar. When simmering, carefully crack the eggs and drop them into the water. Cook for 2–3 minutes on a very gentle simmer, or until the eggs are cooked to your liking. Remove with a slotted spoon.

5 To serve: divide the bubble and squeak between 4 plates and top each portion with a poached egg.

Per serving: **calories:** 298 **fat:** 19.7g **saturated fat:** 9.2g **carbohydrate:** 20.3g **protein:** 11.2g **fibre:** 2.6g **salt:** 0.42g

Preparation: 10 minutes **Cooking:** 25–30 minutes **Serves** 4

watercress burgers

1 bulb of garlic, unpeeled
1 teaspoon olive oil
1 (85g) bag watercress
675g/1¹/₂lb lean minced beef
1 tablespoon Dijon mustard
salt and ground black pepper
4 buns

For the watercress butter:
1 (85g) bag watercress
100g/4oz unsalted butter
1 shallot, finely chopped
2 anchovy fillets
2 tablespoons ground almonds

1 Preheat the oven to 180°C/Fan 160°C/Gas Mark 4. Cut the top off the bulb of garlic and drizzle over the olive oil, then bake for 20 minutes, or until the garlic is tender. Cool, then separate the cloves of garlic and squeeze the pulp from each: place in a bowl.

2 Whilst the garlic roasts, make the watercress butter: finely chop the watercress and mash into the butter with the shallot, anchovies and almonds. Season with pepper. Roll the butter in greaseproof paper to form a sausage shape, and freeze for 20 minutes.

3 Make the burgers: finely chop half the watercress and mix with the roasted garlic, minced beef and mustard. Season with salt and plenty of ground black pepper. Divide into 4 portions and shape each one into a 2.5cm/1in thick burger. Cut the chilled watercress butter into 4 pieces. Make an indentation in each burger and place a nugget of butter in the centre. Shape the mince to enclose the butter inside the burger. Chill in the fridge until ready to cook.

4 Grill, pan-fry, griddle or barbecue the burgers to your liking, turning once: 4 minutes each side for rare; 6 minutes each side for medium; 8 minutes each side for well done. Set aside to stand for 5 minutes.

5 Split the buns and toast the insides. Fill them with the burgers and remaining watercress leaves.

Per serving: calories: 687 fat: 44.6g saturated fat: 21.1g
carbohydrate: 27.3g protein: 45.9g fibre: 2.4g salt: 1.63g

Preparation: 20 minutes plus chilling Cooking: 30-35 minutes Serves 4

watercress, bacon and egg wraps

4 large eggs, hard-boiled and roughly chopped
1 gherkin, chopped
100g/4oz ready-made potato salad
2 rashers crispy bacon, crumbled
2 x 23cm/9in soft flour tortillas
50g/2oz watercress

For the watercress butter:
1 (85g) bag watercress, finely chopped
75g/3oz unsalted butter, softened
1 shallot, very finely chopped
1 teaspoon English mustard
freshly ground black pepper

1 Make the watercress butter: in a bowl, mix the watercress, butter, shallot and mustard together with a fork. Season well with freshly ground black pepper. Keep at room temperature.

2 Make the filling: in a clean bowl, mix the hard-boiled eggs together with the gherkin, potato salad and bacon until thoroughly mixed.

3 Lay the two tortillas out on a clean work surface and dab each one with a little watercress butter. Cover with the egg filling, leaving a 2.5cm/1in border. Top with the watercress.

4 Roll up the tortillas tightly, folding over the edges as you do so to enclose the filling. Either cut in half or leave whole. Wrap them tightly in clingfilm ready for the lunchbox.

Cook's tip
You do not need to use all the watercress butter – any leftovers will make a delicious sandwich filling. Alternatively, keep some wrapped in foil in the fridge and cut a slice off to place on top of a poached salmon or white fish fillet.

Per serving: calories: 657 fat: 40.2g saturated fat: 12.2g
carbohydrate: 45.2g protein: 31.5g fibre: 2.5g salt: 3.56g

Preparation: 5 minutes Serves 2

watercress and red pepper pancakes

1 tablespoon olive oil
1 small shallot, finely chopped
25g/1oz mushrooms, sliced
1 large egg
100ml/4fl oz milk
25g/1oz watercress leaves
25g/1oz plain flour
salt and ground black pepper
pinch of ground allspice

For the filling:
225g/8oz soured cream
1 tablespoon lemon juice
75g/3oz mushrooms, sliced
2 roasted peppers, peeled and diced
1 (85g) bag watercress

1 Make the pancake batter: heat the oil in a small pan, add the shallot and mushrooms and sauté for 2 minutes until golden. Cool slightly. Place the mushroom and shallots, egg, milk, watercress, flour, salt, pepper and allspice in a food processor and blend until smooth. Pour into a jug and leave to stand for 10 minutes.

2 To cook the pancakes, line a plate with 2 sheets of kitchen paper and set aside. Lightly brush a small frying pan with a little of the oil, then place the pan over a medium heat until hot. Remove from the heat and pour about 3 tablespoons of the batter into the centre of the pan. Quickly tilt the pan in all directions to evenly coat the base. Cook over a medium heat for 1–2 minutes or until golden underneath. Flip the pancake over onto the other side and continue cooking until golden. Flip out onto the kitchen paper and cover with another sheet of kitchen paper. Repeat to make about 6 pancakes in total.

3 Make the filling: beat the soured cream and the lemon juice until light. Add the mushrooms, peppers and watercress and lightly mix. Season to taste. Lay the cooked pancakes out on a work surface and divide the filling between them, spooning it down the centre of each. Roll up and place in a lightly buttered shallow dish.

4 Bake the pancakes in a preheated oven at 190°C/Fan 170°C/ Gas Mark 5 for about 10 minutes. Serve hot with watercress salad.

Cook's tip
Roasted peppers are available in cans or jars from supermarkets. They have all the skin and seeds removed, ready for use.

Per serving: calories: 174 fat: 14.2g saturated fat: 5.8g carbohydrate: 7.6g protein: 4.5g fibre: 1.1g salt: 0.58g

Preparation: 25 minutes Cooking: 10 minutes Serves 6

watercress farming

Watercress is a semi-aquatic plant and on UK farms it grows in the most idyllic circumstances, alongside streams and rivers near where the springs rise. Farmers harness this water directly from the spring deep underground, and channel it to flow through their shallow gravel watercress beds.

The water is introduced gently at first and then in ever-increasing volumes as the plants grow, up to a maximum depth of two inches, with a mature bed needing up to 20,000 gallons of flowing water per acre per hour. The beds are gently sloping as it is imperative that watercress grows in flowing water. The water is only 'borrowed' as once its work is done, it is allowed to flow back on its original course towards the river.

The first British watercress farm was developed in 1808 in Northfleet, near Gravesend, in Kent. The industry spread along the chalk downs, which run from Dorset up through the Home Counties to Lincolnshire. The capillary-like structure of chalk acts like a natural sponge and can hold vast quantities of water in underground pressurised aquifers, before the water finds a fault and rises to the surface as a natural spring. The South of England landscape provides a constant supply of crystal-

Miniature railway for transporting watercress from the farm in the 1940s.

clear spring water which rises from the ground at a constant 10–11°C, just right for protecting the crop during the winter and cooling it in summer. On a winter's day steam can be seen rising from the beds as the warmer spring water meets the cold air and the watercress retreats close to the water surface to keep warm.

Watercress is a member of the healthy *Cruciferae* (or *Brassicaceae*) family, and is related to broccoli, cabbage, brussels sprouts, cauliflower, rocket and radish – it should not be confused with mustard and cress, a different species. Watercress is available all year round, produced in the UK from March to November. In the winter, home-grown watercress can be unreliable, so some producers have farms overseas for a year-round supply.

The beautiful Georgian town of Alresford in Hampshire is renowned as the UK's 'capital of watercress farming' and celebrates the British watercress season every May with The Watercress Festival. The first of the harvest is delivered by horse and cart and visitors can take guided tours of the watercress farms. The Watercress Line steam train, which used to transport watercress to Covent Garden Market, still runs, but today it carries tourists rather than watercress.

Although there have been huge advances in the harvesting, packaging and distribution of watercress, it is a refreshing thought that the way the plant is grown has hardly changed in the last 200 years.

mackerel and watercress salad

2 large oranges
225g/8oz smoked mackerel fillets with peppercorns
2 chicory heads, trimmed
1 (85g) bag watercress
1 tablespoon olive oil
2 teaspoons wholegrain mustard
1 teaspoon clear honey
salt and ground black pepper

1 Use a sharp knife to remove the peel from one orange, cutting away all the white pith. Then cut between the white membranes to separate the orange segments. Take the second orange and squeeze its juice into a bowl. Set aside.

2 Remove the skin from the smoked mackerel fillets and cut the flesh into bite-sized pieces. Separate the chicory into leaves. Arrange the watercress, chicory, mackerel and orange segments in a large salad bowl.

3 Whisk the reserved orange juice with the olive oil, mustard and honey. Season with a little salt and freshly ground black pepper. Drizzle over the salad and serve immediately.

Cook's tip
Watercress and orange are the perfect nutritional combination as the vitamin C in the orange helps our bodies to absorb the valuable iron in the peppery watercress. And, of course, watercress also contains vitamin C.

Per serving: calories: 272 fat: 21g saturated fat: 4.6g
carbohydrate: 8.9g protein: 12.5g fibre: 2g salt: 1.21g

Preparation: 10 minutes Serves 4

red pepper and goat's cheese salad

1 red pepper

1 red onion, sliced

2 tablespoons pine nuts

1 tablespoon olive oil

2 teaspoons balsamic vinegar

1 (85g) bag watercress

1 x 50g/2oz chêvre goat's cheese, crumbled

salt and ground black pepper

1 Preheat the oven to 220°C/ Fan 200°C/ Gas Mark 6. Place the whole red pepper on the middle shelf of the oven and roast for 20 minutes, or until the skin has begun to brown.

2 Meanwhile, toss the red onion, pine nuts and olive oil together on a small baking tray and then roast for 10 minutes. Stir the vinegar and salt and pepper into the onion mixture and set aside.

3 Carefully remove the pepper from the oven and place in a plastic bag. Leave to cool - this helps 'sweat' the skin off the pepper. Peel away the skin and remove the seeds. Slice the flesh into strips.

4 Place the watercress in a salad bowl. Add the goat's cheese, sliced red pepper, onion, pine nuts and any pan juices. Toss lightly to mix together and serve with some crusty bread.

Per serving: calories: 220 fat: 15.5g saturated fat: 5.3g
carbohydrate: 11.1g protein: 9.7g fibre: 2.9g salt: 0.51g

Preparation: 10 minutes   Cooking: 20 minutes Serves 2

thai-style beef and watercress salad

2 (175g/6oz) sirloin steaks, trimmed of fat

1 tablespoon Szechuan peppercorns, crushed

3 tomatoes, deseeded and sliced

1 small red onion, thinly sliced

225g/8oz cucumber, peeled, deseeded and sliced

1 (85g) bag watercress

2 tablespoons Thai sweet chilli dipping sauce

juice of 1 lime

1 tablespoon Thai fish sauce

salt

1 Coat the sirloin steaks with the crushed peppercorns, pressing them in well, and then season with a little salt. Cook the steaks under a hot grill for 6-8 minutes, turning them once, until medium rare. Set aside for 2 minutes to cool slightly.

2 In a bowl, toss the tomatoes, red onion and cucumber with the watercress. Whisk the sweet chilli sauce, lime juice and fish sauce together until blended.

3 Thinly slice the warm steaks and toss together with the salad and dressing. Serve immediately with some crusty bread.

Cook's tip
Szechuan peppercorns are sold with the spices in supermarkets. They add a fragrant oriental flavour to this dish, but if you haven't got any, use black peppercorns instead.

Per serving: calories: 159 fat: 4.6g saturated fat: 1.6g
carbohydrate: 7.1g protein: 22.9g fibre: 1.5g salt: 0.88g

Preparation: 10 minutes Cooking: 6-8 minutes Serves 4

watercress, mango and chicken salad

150g/5oz asparagus tips
1 mango, peeled and stoned
100g/4oz red seedless grapes
350g/12oz cooked chicken breast
1 (85g) bag watercress
3 tablespoons pumpkin seeds

For the dressing:
grated zest and juice of 1 orange
1/2 teaspoon dried chilli flakes
1 teaspoon honey
salt and ground black pepper

1 Cook the asparagus tips in a saucepan of boiling water for 2 minutes. Drain in a colander and refresh them in cold water.

2 Thinly slice the mango flesh and halve the grapes. Cut the chicken breast into bite-sized pieces.

3 Place the asparagus, mango, grapes and chicken in a serving bowl. Add the watercress and pumpkin seeds.

4 Place all the dressing ingredients in a jug and whisk together with a fork until well blended. Drizzle the dressing over the salad and lightly toss until everything is coated. Serve immediately.

Cook's tip
You could substitute 2 ripe peaches or nectarines or even a papaya for the mango in this salad.

Per serving: calories: 275 fat: 8.9g saturated fat: 2.2g
carbohydrate: 18.2g protein: 31.7g fibre: 3.3g salt: 0.17g

Preparation: 10 minutes Cooking: 2 minutes Serves 4

watercress tabbouleh

100g/4oz bulgur wheat

2 (85g) bags watercress

4 ripe tomatoes, deseeded and chopped

4 spring onions, trimmed and chopped

juice of 1 lemon

3 tablespoons olive oil

salt and ground black pepper

little gem lettuce leaves, to serve

1 Place the bulgur wheat in a large bowl and pour boiling water over the top. Cover the bowl with a plate and then leave to stand for about 15 minutes. The grains will swell and absorb most of the liquid. Drain off any excess liquid.

2 Reserve a handful of the watercress and finely chop the remainder. Stir the chopped watercress, tomatoes, spring onions, lemon juice and olive oil into the bulgur wheat and season to taste with salt and pepper.

3 Leave to marinate for at least 20 minutes to allow the flavours to develop. Line a serving bowl with some little gem lettuce leaves and the reserved sprigs of watercress. Spoon the tabbouleh into the centre and serve. This is particularly delicious served with barbecued chicken.

Cook's tip
This North African salad works equally well with couscous. Just follow the directions on the packet and combine with the salad.

Per serving: calories: 184 fat: 9.4g saturated fat: 1.3g carbohydrate: 22.0g protein: 4.4g fibre: 1.5g salt: 0.07g

Preparation: 10 minutes + soaking Marinating: 20 minutes Serves 4

watercress, tuna and bean salad

225g/8oz cucumber

3 ripe tomatoes

1 (410g) can cannellini beans, drained

1 (200g) can tuna chunks in spring water, drained

2 tablespoons fat-free French-style dressing

1 (85g) bag watercress

salt and ground black pepper

1 Thickly slice the cucumber and then cut each slice into quarters. Cut the tomatoes roughly into chunks. In a bowl, mix the cucumber and tomatoes with the cannellini beans and tuna chunks.

2 Drizzle the French-style dressing over the bean and tuna mixture and then toss together with the watercress leaves. Check the seasoning and serve immediately with some crusty bread.

Cook's tip
This makes a splendid, healthy summer lunch. If you don't have any cannellini beans in your store cupboard, you can use canned haricot, flageolet or butter beans instead.

Per serving: calories: 127 fat: 1.3g saturated fat: 0.1g
carbohydrate: 15.4g protein: 14.6g fibre: 4.6g salt: 1.01g

Preparation: 5 minutes Serves 4

spiced squash and watercress soup

1 tablespoon olive oil

1 onion, chopped

900g/2lb butternut squash, washed, deseeded and cut into chunks

1/2 teaspoon dried chilli flakes

600ml/1 pint vegetable stock

1 (85g) bag watercress, roughly chopped

3 tablespoons crème fraîche

salt and ground black pepper

watercress sprigs, to garnish

1 Heat the oil in a large saucepan, then add the onion and sauté for about 2 minutes. Add the squash, stir well and then cover the pan with a lid. Cook for 2 minutes.

2 Stir in the chilli flakes and vegetable stock, then bring to the boil. Cover the pan and simmer gently for 15 minutes, or until the butternut squash is cooked and tender.

3 Transfer the soup to a blender and blitz, in batches, until smooth. Return the soup to the saucepan and add the watercress and crème fraîche. Season to taste with salt and ground black pepper.

4 Gently reheat the soup before ladling into serving bowls. Garnish with sprigs of watercress and serve with crusty bread.

Per serving: calories: 169 fat: 8g saturated fat: 3.3g carbohydrate: 21.0g protein: 4g fibre: 4.9g salt: 0.25g

Preparation: 10 minutes Cooking: 20 minutes Serves 4

watercress soup

1 tablespoon olive oil

1 small onion, chopped

1 small stick celery, chopped

350g/12oz potatoes, peeled and diced

600ml/1 pint chicken or vegetable stock

3 (85g) bags watercress

150ml/¼ pint milk

pinch of ground nutmeg

squeeze of lemon juice

salt and ground black pepper

1 Heat the oil in a large pan. Add the onion and celery and sauté over a medium heat for 5 minutes until pale golden. Stir in the potatoes and stock and then bring to the boil. Cover and simmer for 10 minutes or until the potatoes are tender.

2 Stir in the watercress, cover the pan and cook for a further 5 minutes or until the watercress is wilted. Transfer the soup to a food processor or blender and blitz until smooth.

3 Rinse out the pan and pour in the puréed soup. Add the milk, nutmeg, lemon juice and seasoning to taste. Gently reheat the soup until piping hot and serve with crusty bread.

Cook's tip

There are lots of variations to this lovely soup. To make Fresh Pea and Watercress Soup, just substitute the potatoes with 400g/14oz of frozen peas and leave out the celery, nutmeg and lemon juice. Serve with a sprig of mint.

Per serving: calories: 167 fat: 5.5g saturated fat: 0.8g carbohydrate: 19.5g protein: 11.1g fibre: 2.7g salt: 0.91g

Preparation: 5 minutes Cooking: 15 minutes Serves 4

watercress, potato and bacon frittata

350g/12oz new potatoes

1 tablespoon olive oil

4 rashers back bacon, trimmed and sliced

1 onion, sliced

1 (85g) bag watercress, roughly chopped

6 eggs

50g/2oz mature Cheddar cheese, grated

salt and ground black pepper

tomato salsa and salad, to serve

1 Cook the new potatoes in a pan of boiling salted water for 10 minutes, or until tender. Drain and slice.

2 Heat the oil in a non-stick frying pan, add the bacon and onion and fry for 3–4 minutes until beginning to brown. Add the sliced potatoes and cook for a further 5 minutes. Add the watercress to the pan and continue to cook for 2 minutes, stirring until it has wilted.

3 Beat the eggs with a little salt and plenty of ground black pepper. Pour the mixture into the pan and then cook, stirring for 1 minute, until most of the egg has set. Shake the pan gently to level the surface and cook for a further 2 minutes.

4 Sprinkle the cheese over the top of the frittata and cook under a hot grill for 2 minutes until the cheese has melted and the top is golden brown. Serve in wedges with tomato salsa and a watercress salad.

Cook's tip
This tasty supper dish is also great served cold in lunchboxes or for picnics. If preparing it for vegetarians, omit the bacon and replace with 1 large sliced red pepper, adding 1 more tablespoon of olive oil to the pan.

Per serving: calories: 319 fat: 19.2g saturated fat: 6.4g
carbohydrate: 16.7g protein: 21g fibre: 1.6g salt: 1.55g

Preparation: 5 minutes Cooking: 25–30 minutes Serves 4

brie, ham and watercress calzone

1 (290g) pack pizza base mix

1 small red onion, thinly sliced

150g/5oz piece of brie, sliced

90g/3oz Parma ham, torn into pieces

1 (85g) bag watercress

salt and ground black pepper

1 Preheat the oven to 230°C/Fan 210°C/Gas Mark 7. Put the pizza dough mix in a bowl and add 200ml/7fl oz warm water. Mix together and then, on a clean work surface, knead to a smooth dough.

2 Divide the dough into 4 pieces. Roll out each portion on a lightly floured surface into a circle, about 23cm/9in diameter.

3 Top one side of each dough circle with the red onion, brie, Parma ham and, finally, the watercress. Season lightly with salt and pepper.

4 Use your fingers to wet the edge of the dough with water. Fold and stretch the dough over to enclose the filling. Pinch and twist the edges together to seal, making a twisted point at each corner of the calzone.

5 Transfer the calzones to a baking sheet and lightly dust with flour. Bake for 10–15 minutes on the top shelf of the preheated oven until they are pale golden. Serve warm with salad.

Per serving: calories: 384 fat: 15.7g saturated fat: 7.8g carbohydrate: 42.2g protein: 21.3g fibre: 4.1g salt: 3.49g

Preparation: 15 minutes Cooking: 10–15 minutes Serves 4

10 great reasons
to eat watercress

Enjoying a wide variety of foods in a balanced diet is key to good health. Some foods, such as watercress, have been classed as 'superfoods' because they are rich in health-promoting nutrients, antioxidants or phytochemicals (bioactive plant compounds). Scientists are still discovering exciting new evidence of the beneficial effects of watercress on human health.

1 Apples, broccoli and tomatoes are often cited as the 'wonder' fruit and vegetables but watercress is a better source of vitamins C, B1, B6, K and E, iron, calcium, magnesium, manganese and zinc. Only raw broccoli has more vitamin C and magnesium – however, it is much more often eaten cooked.

2 For an energy boost, blend an 85g bag of watercress with 150ml fresh orange juice, 100ml carrot juice, 100ml tomato juice and a dash of Tabasco. Liquidise, pour into a glass and garnish with a carrot stick.

3 Watercress is believed by many people to be an aphrodisiac. In Crete, for example, the islanders swear by its powers and ancient recipes are handed down from one generation to the next.

4 Watercress literally oozes beta-carotene, which is needed for healthy skin and eyes. No wonder the seventeenth-century philosopher and statesman Francis Bacon claimed that it could 'restore a youthful bloom to women'.

5 According to legend, watercress grew in the springs of the Dikton Cave on Crete where the god Zeus is reputed to have eaten the plant in order to fortify himself against his murderous father Cronos.

6 Watercress provides iodine and most B vitamins, including folic acid which is extremely important for a healthy pregnancy and increasing a woman's chances of having a healthy baby.

7 Watercress is said to be a good cure for a hangover. For a great 'morning after' cocktail, peel and dice one mango and whizz in a blender with 1 bag of watercress and up to 500ml pure apple juice.

8 Watercress contains Lutein and Zeaxanthin, types of carotenoids that act as antioxidants, meaning that they can mop up potentially damaging free radicals. Lutein specifically is considered to be very important for healthy eyes. It also contains Quercetin, a type of flavonoid and a powerful antioxidant.

9 The ancient Greeks called watercress *kardamon*; they believed that it could brighten their intellect, and hence their proverb 'Eat watercress and get wit'.

10 Watercress is low in calories and fat. A serving of 80g (or a cereal bowlful) has just 18 calories and makes up one of the five daily portions of fruit and vegetables, as recommended by health experts.

potato, feta and watercress pastries

450g/1lb potatoes, peeled and chopped

1 (85g) bag watercress, roughly chopped

1 tablespoon chopped fresh mint

200g/7oz feta cheese, drained and crumbled

10 sheets filo pastry

4 tablespoons olive oil

salt and ground black pepper

1 Cook the potatoes in a large pan of boiling salted water for about 15 minutes until just tender. Drain thoroughly and then 'dry' in the saucepan over gentle heat.

2 Roughly mash the potatoes, then stir in the watercress and leave to cool. Stir in the mint and feta and season to taste with salt and pepper.

3 Work with one sheet of filo pastry at a time, keeping the others covered with cling film and a damp tea towel. Brush the pastry lightly with olive oil on one side and cut into 3 long strips.

4 Preheat the oven to 200°C/Fan 180°C/Gas Mark 6. Place a spoonful of the filling at one end of a pastry strip. Fold the corner of the pastry over the filling, so that the top edge of the pastry is over the right edge. Take the point of the strip and fold it down towards the bottom of the pastry to create a triangle shape. Continue folding the pastry in this way and brushing with any remaining oil. Repeat to make 17 more triangles in the same way.

5 Place the pastry triangles on a baking sheet and then bake in the preheated oven for 20 minutes, or until they are crisp and golden brown. Serve them fresh and warm from the oven.

Per serving: calories: 100 fat: 5.1g saturated fat: 1.8g carbohydrate: 11.0g protein: 3.2g fibre: 0.4g salt: 0.67g

Preparation: 30 minutes Cooking: 20 minutes Makes: 18

watercress and pea risotto

1 tablespoon olive oil

1 onion, finely chopped

1 clove garlic, crushed

350g/12oz risotto rice

150ml/¼ pint dry white wine

750ml/1¼ pints hot vegetable stock

150g/5oz frozen peas

½ teaspoon freshly grated nutmeg

1 (85g) bag watercress, roughly chopped

25g/1oz freshly grated parmesan cheese

salt and ground black pepper

1 Heat the oil in a large heavy frying pan. Add the onion and sauté for 4 minutes until soft but not coloured. Add the garlic and rice and cook for 1 more minute, stirring.

2 Add the white wine and cook, stirring, for 2–3 minutes until most of the liquid has been absorbed. Add a ladle of the hot stock and cook for 2–3 minutes, gently stirring occasionally to prevent the rice sticking. When the liquid has been absorbed, add a little more stock. Repeat until you have just a little stock left and the rice is almost tender.

3 Add the remaining stock, peas and nutmeg. Cook until the rice is soft and creamy, then remove the pan from the heat.

4 Add the watercress and parmesan cheese, and season to taste with salt and pepper. Serve the risotto immediately. This is especially delicious eaten with grilled fish or chicken.

Per serving: calories: 456 fat: 6.5g saturated fat: 1.9g
carbohydrate: 87.7g protein: 14g fibre: 5.3g salt: 0.41g

Preparation: 10 minutes Cooking: 25 minutes Serves 4

stuffed peppers

25g/1oz brown basmati rice

1 each red, orange and yellow peppers

1 (85g) bag watercress, roughly chopped

50g/2oz pitted black olives, chopped

50g/2oz drained sun-dried tomatoes

50g/2oz Cheddar cheese, grated

salt and ground black pepper

salad, to serve

1 Cook the brown rice in a large pan of boiling salted water for about 20 minutes until tender but retaining some 'bite'. Alternatively, cook according to the packet instructions. Drain well.

2 Preheat the oven to 200°C/Fan180°C/Gas Mark 6. Cut the peppers in half lengthways, cutting through the stalks. Remove the seeds and discard them. Place the peppers cut-side up in a roasting tin.

3 Mix the rice, watercress, olives and sun-dried tomatoes together with half the grated Cheddar cheese. Season to taste with salt and pepper. Spoon the mixture into the pepper halves, and scatter the remaining cheese over the top.

4 Bake the peppers in the preheated oven for 25–30 minutes, or until they are cooked and tender. Serve hot with salad.

Cook's tip
This is a very versatile dish and you can vary the rice filling by adding chopped ripe tomatoes, mushrooms or spring onions.

Per serving: **calories:** 99 **fat:** 6.0g **saturated fat:** 2.2g **carbohydrate:** 7.7g **protein:** 4.0g **fibre:** 2.6g **salt:** 0.64g

Preparation: 10 minutes   **Cooking:** 45–50 minutes **Serves** 6

watercress pesto linguine

350g/12oz linguine or pappardelle
1 small clove garlic
25g/1oz pine nuts
1 tablespoon capers
25g/1oz parmesan cheese, grated
2 (85g) bags watercress
4 tablespoons olive oil
squeeze of lemon juice
50g/2oz pitted black olives, roughly chopped
150g/5oz cherry tomatoes, halved
salt and ground black pepper

1 Cook the pasta in a large pan of boiling salted water for 10 minutes, or according to the packet instructions, until just tender and *al dente*.

2 Make the pesto: whilst the pasta is cooking, place the garlic, pine nuts and capers in a food processor or blender and blend until finely chopped. Add the parmesan cheese and watercress, reserving a handful of leaves for the garnish, and blitz again. With the motor running, add the olive oil through the feed tube and, finally, the lemon juice. Season to taste with salt and pepper.

3 Drain the pasta well in a colander and then return it to the warm saucepan. Add the pesto, black olives and tomatoes and toss together gently. Stir in the reserved watercress and serve.

Per serving: calories: 509 fat: 21.4g saturated fat: 3.7g
carbohydrate: 68.2g protein: 15.4g fibre: 4.5g salt: 0.48g

Preparation: 30 minutes Cooking: 20 minutes Serves 4

penne with watercress and salmon

350g/12oz penne

4 x 75g/3oz salmon fillets

1 (200ml) tub crème fraîche

grated zest and juice of 1 lemon

2 teaspoons pesto sauce*

1 x (85g) bag watercress, roughly chopped

salt and ground black pepper

1 Cook the pasta in a large pan of lightly salted boiling water for about 8–10 minutes, or according to the packet instructions, until *al dente*.

2 Meanwhile, place the salmon in a frying pan, skin-side up, add 100ml/4fl oz water and cover with a lid. Slowly bring to the boil and then simmer gently for about 5 minutes or until the salmon is cooked. (Alternatively, if you have a microwave, place the salmon, skin-side up, on a heatproof plate and cook for 4 minutes on high. Leave to stand for 2 minutes). Remove the skin and flake the flesh.

3 Place the crème fraîche in a small pan, add the lemon zest and juice and pesto and bring to the boil. Simmer uncovered for 5 minutes, or until reduced slightly. Season to taste with salt and pepper.

4 Drain the pasta, and add the watercress, salmon and crème fraîche. Toss well to mix and then divide between 4 serving plates. Serve topped with a sprig of watercress.

Per serving: calories: 643 fat: 30.7g saturated fat: 15.1g carbohydrate: 68g protein: 28g fibre: 3.1g salt: 0.20g

Preparation: 5 minutes Cooking: 20 minutes Serves 4

* See page 49 for fresh pesto

gnocchi with pancetta and watercress

1 tablespoon olive oil

75g/3oz cubed pancetta or streaky bacon

1 clove garlic, chopped

4 ripe tomatoes, chopped

$1/_2$ teaspoon dried chilli flakes

4 tablespoons dry white wine

pinch of sugar

1 (85g) bag watercress

1 (500g) bag fresh potato gnocchi

watercress and shaved parmesan cheese, to serve

1 Heat the oil in a frying pan, add the pancetta and sauté for 5 minutes, or until golden and all the fat has run out. Add the garlic and tomatoes, and sauté for 2 minutes, then add the chilli flakes, wine and sugar. Cover the pan and simmer for 5 minutes.

2 Place the watercress on a board and use a sharp knife to chop it very roughly; place the watercress in a colander.

3 Cook the potato gnocchi in a large pan of lightly salted boiling water according to the packet instructions. Drain the gnocchi in the colander, pouring it on top of the watercress. Leave to drain for 1 minute before tossing into the hot tomato sauce.

4 Serve the gnocchi topped with a little more watercress and some parmesan shavings.

Per serving: calories: 297 fat: 8.5g saturated fat: 2.5g
carbohydrate: 45.6g protein: 10.1g fibre: 3.0g salt: 2.27g

Preparation: 5 minutes Cooking: 10–15 minutes Serves 4

10 easy ways
with watercress

While watercress is a classic ingredient in soups, salads and sandwiches, its repertoire is endlessly versatile, adding a tangy bite and a generous sprinkling of vitamins and minerals to a range of everyday dishes.

1 Watercress is a staple food among the Chinese, who believe that it brings the body back into balance, holistically and nutritionally. It's great in stir fries – throw it in at the last minute and cook until just wilted.

2 Fed up with plain old mashed potato? Why not add a peeled clove of garlic to the potatoes while they boil, then drain and mash with a knob of butter and a spoonful or two of wholegrain mustard? Stir through a bag of roughly chopped watercress and plenty of ground black pepper.

3 The distinctive mustardy flavour of watercress makes it the perfect partner to eggs. Use it in a classic omelette with a sprinkling of freshly grated parmesan cheese, or stir into softly scrambled eggs just before serving.

4 An effective and delicious way to increase your vegetable intake is to empty a bag of chopped watercress into a pan of pasta just before serving. Try it and see for yourself.

5 Watercress perks up any sandwich, adding both flavour and crunch. A favourite is with Marmite.

6 In France, roasts were traditionally served with gravy made from pressed watercress juice. An easier way is to serve your roast on a bed of watercress – it's great for mopping up the gravy and meat juices.

7 Watercress mayonnaise is delicious with some poached salmon, asparagus or as a dip. Tip a bag of watercress into a blender with a handful of parsley and blitz. Stir in 10 tablespoons of mayonnaise, 2 tablespoons of soured cream or natural yoghurt and a teaspoon of Dijon mustard.

8 For a classic fish sauce, sauté 2 chopped shallots and a celery stick with butter. Pop in a bay leaf, $^{1}/_{2}$ glass dry white wine, $^{1}/_{4}$ pint stock and simmer for 5 minutes. Add $^{1}/_{4}$ pint crème fraîche and simmer until reduced and slightly thickened. Add 2 bags of chopped watercress and heat through. Liquidise for a smoother version.

9 Instead of salsa verde, blitz a bag of watercress, a handful of basil leaves, 1 garlic clove, 2 tablespoons lemon juice and 2 teaspoons olive oil in a food processor until smooth. Season and serve with chargrilled tuna.

10 For posh peas with the Sunday roast, cook some shallots until soft. Add garlic, watercress, peas, fresh thyme and sugar, then boiling water. Cook for 5 minutes. Drain the peas, remove the thyme and stir in some crème fraîche.

fish and shellfish

teriyaki salmon

4 (100g/4oz) salmon fillets
2.5cm/1in root ginger, peeled
6 spring onions, trimmed
1 stalk lemongrass, trimmed
8 tablespoons teriyaki sauce
1 (85g) bag watercress

1 Preheat the oven to 190°C/Fan 170°C/Gas Mark 5. Place the salmon fillets in the centre of 4 squares of kitchen foil. Finely shred the ginger, spring onions and lemongrass and then scatter them over the salmon fillets. Drizzle 2 tablespoons teriyaki sauce over each one.

2 Fold the foil over the salmon and vegetables, crinkling the edges together to seal them, and make 4 parcels. Place the foil parcels on a baking tray and then place in the preheated oven for 10–15 minutes, or until they are cooked in the centre.

3 To serve, divide the watercress between 4 serving plates. Remove the salmon and vegetables from the foil parcels and place on top of the watercress with the cooking juices. Serve with new potatoes.

Cook's tip
You can cook other fish in this way. This cooking method prevents the fish drying out and avoids smells in the kitchen. Experiment with plaice or sole fillets, or even tuna or swordfish.

Per serving: calories: 237 fat: 26g saturated fat: 2g
carbohydrate: 14g protein: 2.7g fibre: 0.9g salt: 2g

Preparation: 10 minutes Cooking: 10–15 minutes Serves 4

watercress garlic dip with prawns

1 tablespoon olive oil

1 shallot, chopped

1 clove garlic, crushed

1 potato, peeled and chopped

100m/4fl oz dry white wine

pinch of chilli flakes

2 (85g) bags watercress

squeeze of lemon juice

4 tablespoons half-fat crème fraîche

salt and pepper

450g/1lb large unshelled raw tiger prawns

wedges of lemon, to serve

1 Heat the oil in a frying pan, then add the shallot and sauté over a gentle heat for 5 minutes, until softened. Stir in the garlic, potato, white wine and chilli flakes, then cover the pan and simmer for 10 minutes, or until the potato is cooked and tender.

2 Add the watercress and cook, stirring for about 4 minutes, by which time the leaves should have wilted. Allow to cool.

3 Add the lemon juice and crème fraîche and then transfer the mixture to a blender or food processor and blitz until smooth. Season to taste with salt and pepper and spoon into a bowl.

4 Brush the tiger prawns with a little oil and then cook on a preheated ridged grill pan or barbecue or under a hot grill, turning them once, until they are pink, cooked through and slightly charred. Serve hot with the watercress garlic dip and lemon wedges.

Cook's tip
This delicious dip complements any barbecued or grilled fish and meat, or you can serve it cold with pitta bread.

Per serving (dip only): **calories:** 97 **fat:** 5.5g **saturated fat:** 1.8g **carbohydrate:** 7.7g **protein:** 2.5g **fibre:** 1.1g **salt:** 0.08g

Preparation: 10 minutes **Cooking:** 15 minutes **Serves** 4

watercress stuffed sole

1 tablespoon olive oil

4 spring onions, sliced

2 (85g) bags watercress, roughly chopped

2 tablespoons crème fraîche

1/2 teaspoon freshly grated nutmeg

8 small lemon sole fillets, skinned

2 tablespoons wholemeal breadcrumbs

2 tablespoons freshly grated parmesan cheese

salt and ground black pepper

1 Preheat the oven to 200°C/Fan 180°C/Gas Mark 6. Heat the oil in a large pan, add the spring onions and watercress and cook over a high heat for 1 minute. Stir in the crème fraîche and cook for 1 minute, or until the watercress has wilted. Add the nutmeg and season to taste with salt and pepper. Cool slightly.

2 Place the sole fillets skinned-side up on a board and divide the watercress mixture between them, spreading it along the length of each fillet. Roll up the fillets to enclose the filling and then secure them with wooden cocktail sticks. Place them in an ovenproof dish and scatter over the breadcrumbs and parmesan cheese.

3 Bake in the preheated oven for 10 minutes, until the fish is cooked through and opaque in the centre. Remove the cocktail sticks before serving with new potatoes.

Cook's tip
You can use other flat white fish fillets, such as plaice, sea bass or dabs, if you prefer.

Per serving: calories: 222 fat: 10.1g saturated fat: 3.8g
carbohydrate: 3g protein: 29.9g fibre: 1.1g salt: 0.56g

Preparation: 15 minutes Cooking: 10–15 minutes Serves 4

chicken and watercress stir fry

1 tablespoon vegetable oil

3 chicken fillets, sliced

6 spring onions, sliced

2 carrots, peeled and cut into matchsticks

100g/4oz broccoli florets

75g/3oz frozen soy beans

5cm/2ins piece root ginger, grated

1 clove garlic, crushed

1 red chilli, deseeded and chopped

1 (85g) bag watercress, roughly chopped

2 tablespoons low-sodium soy sauce

egg noodles, to serve

1 Heat the oil in a large, deep frying pan or wok. Add the chicken and stir fry briskly over a high heat for 4 minutes, until golden brown all over.

2 Add the spring onions, carrots and broccoli florets, together with 2 tablespoons water and stir fry for 3 minutes, until tender.

3 Stir in the soy beans, ginger, garlic and chilli, and stir fry for 2 minutes, adding a little more water if things begin to stick to the pan.

4 Finally, add the watercress and soy sauce and stir fry for 1 more minute. Serve straight away with egg noodles.

Cook's tip
Instead of chicken, you could add chunks of turkey breast, diced pork or steak, or even raw tiger prawns. They all taste equally good.

Per serving: calories: 190 fat: 5.6g saturated fat: 0.9g
carbohydrate: 7.6g protein: 27.6g fibre: 3.1g salt: 1.03g

Preparation: 10 minutes Cooking: 10 minutes Serves 4

chicken on watercress pappardelle

1 tablespoon olive oil

4 chicken breast fillets

100ml/4fl oz red wine or stock

1 (350g) jar tomato and chilli pasta sauce

225g/8oz pappardelle pasta ribbons

1 (85g) bag watercress, roughly chopped

$^1/_2$ teaspoon freshly grated nutmeg

25g/1oz parmesan cheese, thinly sliced

ground black pepper

1 Heat 1 teaspoon olive oil in a large non-stick frying pan, then add the chicken breast fillets and sauté for 8-10 minutes, turning them once, until browned on both sides.

2 Add the wine (or stock) and simmer for 2–3 minutes, until it has nearly all evaporated. Add the tomato pasta sauce, cover the pan and simmer for 5 minutes, or until the chicken is nearly cooked through.

3 Meanwhile, cook the pasta in a large pan of boiling salted water for 7 minutes, or according to the packet instructions. It should be just *al dente*. Drain in a colander.

4 Put the watercress, nutmeg and remaining oil in the warm pan, add the pasta and toss to mix, seasoning well with black pepper. Keep warm.

5 Arrange the slices of parmesan cheese on top of the chicken and place the frying pan under a hot grill. Cook for 2 minutes, or until the cheese melts and is golden brown. Serve the chicken and sauce on top of the wilted watercress pappardelle.

Cook's tip
Pappardelle pasta is a broad flat noodle; if you prefer, you could use an equal quantity of tagliatelle or linguine in this recipe instead – just adjust the cooking time according to the packet instructions.

Per serving: calories: 472 fat: 10.5g saturated fat: 2.6g
carbohydrate: 48.7g protein: 44.6g fibre: 3.2g salt: 1.33g

Preparation: 5 minutes Cooking: 20 minutes Serves 4

creamy stuffed chicken

50g/2oz soft (medium-fat) cheese

1 (85g) bag watercress, finely chopped

1 small clove garlic, crushed

4 skinless chicken breast fillets

4 slices Parma ham

1 tablespoon olive oil

4 tablespoons Marsala wine

150ml/¼ pint chicken stock

4 tablespoons double cream

salt and ground black pepper

1 Mash the cheese with half the watercress, and the garlic. Season lightly with salt and pepper. Use a sharp knife to make a slit along one side of each chicken breast to make a pocket. Fill with the cheese mixture, then wrap the Parma ham around the chicken, tucking the loose ends of ham underneath.

2 Heat the oil in a frying pan, add the chicken breasts and cook them for about 8 minutes, turning them over once, until the ham is golden brown. Add the Marsala to the pan, cook for 1 minute, and then stir in the chicken stock.

3 Cover the pan with a lid, a baking sheet or some kitchen foil, and simmer gently for 15–20 minutes, or until the chicken is tender and cooked right through.

4 Remove the chicken from the pan and keep warm. Increase the heat and cook the liquid to reduce it. Stir in the remaining watercress and cream and bring to the boil. Simmer for 1 minute, then remove from the heat and season to taste.

5 Serve the chicken in a pool of creamy sauce with some crushed potatoes and green beans.

Cook's tip
You can use sherry as an alternative to Marsala; it will still taste delicious.

Per serving: **calories:** 342 **fat:** 17.5g **saturated fat:** 7.4g **carbohydrate:** 2.0g; **protein:** 41.0g **fibre:** 0.4g **salt:** 1.16g

Preparation: 10 minutes **Cooking:** 30 minutes **Serves** 4

sweet pork and chilli stir fry

1 tablespoon vegetable oil

450g/1lb lean stir fry pork strips

1 red pepper, cored, deseeded and thinly sliced

1 bunch spring onions, trimmed and sliced

1 clove garlic, chopped

2.5cm/1in piece root ginger, grated

1 (85g) bag watercress

2 tablespoons sweet chilli dipping sauce

1 tablespoon fish sauce

noodles or rice, to serve

1 Heat the oil in a large non-stick frying pan or wok, then add the pork strips and stir fry over a high heat for 6–8 minutes, until browned.

2 Add the red pepper, spring onions, garlic and ginger and stir fry for 2–3 minutes until tender.

3 Add the watercress, chilli and fish sauce, and stir fry for 1–2 minutes, or until the watercress leaves have wilted. Serve immediately with some noodles or boiled rice.

Cook's tip
If you prefer, you could use some sliced turkey steaks or chicken breast fillets instead of the pork.

Per serving: calories: 205 fat: 7.8g saturated fat: 1.9g
carbohydrate: 20.3g protein: 11.2g fibre: 2.6g salt: 0.42g

Preparation: 5 minutes Cooking: 10–15 minutes Serves 4

lamb kebabs with watercress couscous

675g/1½lb lamb neck fillet, trimmed

2 tablespoons harissa paste

2 tablespoons olive oil

225g/8oz couscous

grated zest and juice of 1 orange

1 each red, green and yellow pepper, cored and deseeded

1 (85g) bag watercress, roughly chopped

salt and ground black pepper

watercress and wedges of orange, to serve

1 Thickly slice the lamb and place in a bowl with the harissa paste and 1 teaspoon olive oil, tossing well until the lamb is coated. Cover and leave to marinate in the fridge for 2–3 hours. Soak 8 bamboo skewers in water for at least 30 minutes.

2 Place the couscous in a large bowl, and add the orange zest and juice, together with 1 tablespoon olive oil and 450ml/¾ pint boiling water. Season with salt and pepper, then stir in the watercress. Cover the bowl with a plate and set aside for 15 minutes, until the liquid has been absorbed. Fluff up the grains with a fork.

3 Cut the peppers into wedges and toss in the remaining oil. Thread the pepper wedges and marinated lamb onto the soaked skewers.

4 Cook the kebabs over hot barbecue coals or under a hot grill for 10-15 minutes, turning them occasionally, until char-grilled on the outside but still slightly pink inside. Serve the kebabs with the couscous, garnished with watercress sprigs and orange wedges.

Cook's tip

Harissa spice paste is used to flavour many North African, especially Tunisian, dishes. A blend of red chillies, garlic and spices, such as caraway seeds and ground coriander, it is available from most supermarkets where it's sold with the dried spices. It tastes fantastic with these lamb kebabs, but if you prefer milder food, just use 1 teaspoon each of ground cumin and coriander, a crushed garlic clove and the zest and juice of 1 lemon.

Per serving: **calories:** 568 **fat:** 31g **saturated fat:** 12.7g **carbohydrate:** 36g **protein:** 38.1g **fibre:** 2.3g **salt:** 0.43g

Preparation: 10 minutes **Marinating:** 2-3 hours **Cooking:** 10-15 minutes **Serves** 4

recipe index